LESLIE STEPHEN AND MATTHEW ARNOLD AS CRITICS *of* WORDSWORTH

LESLIE STEPHEN AND MATTHEW ARNOLD AS CRITICS *of* WORDSWORTH

by

JOHN DOVER WILSON

THE LESLIE STEPHEN LECTURE DELIVERED
BEFORE THE UNIVERSITY OF CAMBRIDGE
ON 2 MAY 1939

CAMBRIDGE

AT THE UNIVERSITY PRESS

1939

CAMBRIDGE
UNIVERSITY PRESS

University Printing House, Cambridge CB2 8BS, United Kingdom

Published in the United States of America by Cambridge University Press, New York

Cambridge University Press is part of the University of Cambridge.

It furthers the University's mission by disseminating knowledge in the pursuit of education, learning and research at the highest international levels of excellence.

www.cambridge.org
Information on this title: www.cambridge.org/9781107681330

First published 1939
First paperback edition 2014

A catalogue record for this publication is available from the British Library

ISBN 978-1-107-68133-0 Paperback

LESLIE STEPHEN AND MATTHEW ARNOLD AS CRITICS *of* WORDSWORTH

The lecture you are presently to hear was already written when I became aware, to my dismay, that my immediate predecessor, Mr Desmond MacCarthy, had anticipated me by taking Leslie Stephen as the subject of the Leslie Stephen lecture for 1937. But dismay turned to self-congratulation when I read his discourse and saw that, so far from conflicting with or merely repeating him I had, in effect, written a sequel which he might have directly inspired. Two of his observations, in particular, will serve as the text for much that I shall have to say later. "It is impossible to imagine", he writes, "a Matthew Arnold who had never been at Oxford and a Leslie Stephen who had never been at Cambridge"; after which he goes on to define Stephen's literary criticism as "the adventures of the soul of

Cambridge among masterpieces".[1] But Leslie Stephen was more than a Cambridge man, he was a student and don of Trinity Hall. And mine is a privilege denied to Mr Mac-Carthy. For, appointed at a time when the Master of Trinity Hall is Vice-Chancellor of the University, I stand to-day in the college which was Stephen's home for fourteen years and on the dais from which he must I suppose himself have delivered many lectures. Piety, therefore, would have compelled me to address you upon some aspect of Stephen's work, apart from all other considerations.

Of Stephen's connection with Trinity Hall it would be impertinence in me to speak; for I am an outsider, even if, being myself connected with the house over the way, I can claim to be in some sense a neighbour. Nor do I need to remind this audience that, during the reign of the Rev. Leslie Stephen as junior tutor and rowing coach, Trinity Hall for the first time finished head of the river and pro-

[1] Desmond MacCarthy, *Leslie Stephen*, 1937, p. 23.

(6)

duced a senior wrangler. He is said to have "*made* the boat of 1859 which was the pioneer of all Trinity Hall's successes" since.[1] And it is from the senior wrangler, afterwards Sir Robert Romer, Lord Justice of Appeal, that we receive the most intimate picture of him at Cambridge. "Perhaps I can best describe him", Romer writes, "as he appears in my memory, by saying that he was a great athlete in mind and body, with a most generous and affectionate nature. That he was a great athlete in body was apparent to all. With a tall, almost gaunt body, devoid of all superfluous flesh and with muscles like steel, he was, for an amateur, one of the very best walkers and mountain climbers of his day." Yet, Romer continues, "it was not as an athlete even then that he was chiefly distinguished, or that he acquired the great influence that he had over the young men that were under him. What chiefly impressed and affected us was the keen intellect he displayed, coupled with the

[1] *Life of Leslie Stephen*, by F. W. Maitland, p. 58.

(7)

generous enthusiasm he had for the subjects that interested him—and they were many—and above all the warm heart that was apparent to all that knew him".[1]

What the older Fellows thought about him it is difficult to discover; but he must have seemed to the undergraduates the almost perfect tutor. And if anything was needed to set the seal upon their admiration for the sportsman, the scholar and the man, it was supplied by an unconventionality and indifference to appearances which the young always rejoice to find in a don. Stephen, it appears, was one of the founders of athletic sports in the university, and once he made a match with a well-known runner for a race in which *he* should walk two miles while the runner ran three. He was beaten in the last thirty yards, but the finish brought him laurels of a kind. For walking, Romer tells us, "in an old flannel shirt and ordinary trousers... his shirt gradually worked itself up and had

[1] *Life*, p. 57.

(8)

ultimately to be discarded, to the great scandal of some of his brother dons, and to the delight of all the undergraduates and strangers". The scene became famous, and even gave rise to the printing of an elaborate mathematical joke setting forth the problem of the "successive denudations" of "a certain graduate whose regard for appearances varies inversely as his velocity". Equally famous were the grey flannel trousers which he wore on the towing path as he cursed the boat. The said trousers, we are told, were graced "with a large amorphous patch of reddish purple material in the seat thereof", the material having once "formed part of the petticoat of the wife of an Alpine guide", who had been called upon to mend a rent torn by a jagged rock. "This", remarks his biographer, "is the only purple patch with which Sir Leslie Stephen can be charged";[1] which from F. W. Maitland is high praise, indeed.

But as Beowulf's poet has said: "Oft have

[1] *Life*, pp. 61–2.

we heard in the days of yore, how the kings of the Danes won glory, how the athlings wrought mighty deeds of valour." And so, only one more Cambridge reminiscence, this time from Stephen's own pen, as an introduction to what follows. More than thirty years after leaving Trinity Hall, he delivered a lecture, which he called "Forgotten Benefactors", commemorating among others a former student of his, in these words:

Long years ago I knew a young man at college; he was so far from being intellectually eminent that he had great difficulty in passing his examinations; he died from the effects of an accident within a very short time after leaving the university, and hardly any one would now remember his name. He had not the smallest impression that there was anything remarkable about himself, and looked up to his teachers and his more brilliant companions with a loyal admiration which would have made him wonder that they should ever take notice of him. And yet I often thought then, and I believe, in looking back, that I thought rightly, that he was of more real use to his contemporaries than any of the persons to whose influence they would most naturally refer as having affected their development. The secret was a very simple one. Without any special intellectual capacity, he somehow represented a beautiful moral type. He possessed the "simple faith miscalled simplicity", and was so absolutely unselfish, so conspicuously pure in his whole life and conduct, so unsuspicious of evil in others, so sweet and loyal in his nature, that to know him was to have before one's eyes an embodiment of some of the most lovable and really admirable qualities that a human being can possess.... He would have been unfeignedly surprised to hear, what I most sincerely believe to have been the truth, that his tutor owed incomparably more to his living exemplification of what is meant by a character of unblemished purity and simplicity, than he owed to the tutor, whose respectable platitudes he received with unaffected humility.[1]

There speaks the essential Stephen; there glows "the warm heart that was apparent to all that

[1] *Social Rights and Duties*, II, pp. 247–9.

knew him". But his singling out of this particular type for notice reveals something even more about him: it shows him to have been instinctively and passionately of Wordsworth's mind. For the portrait of the unnamed Trinity Hall boy who died in the late fifties or early sixties of last century, though of course not intended to challenge them in the sphere of art, belongs in feeling and emphasis to the same school as *Michael*, *The Old Cumberland Beggar*, *The Leech-gatherer* and other figures in Wordsworth's gallery.

He resembled Wordsworth too in his passion for truth as he saw it, in his almost stark integrity of mind, and above all in his profound moral sense. For though, as we shall see, intensely disliking cant and always ready to smile at moral priggery, he was himself to sacrifice too much to conscience to regard it as anything but one of the great realities. A nature like his was indeed bound to suffer. And the crisis which Wordsworth describes in the tenth book of *The Prelude* finds its parallel in the years, to him years of anguish, during which Stephen, having discovered that he could no longer live as a clergyman, gave up first his tutorship and then his beloved home in this college. He stole out of Cambridge at the beginning of 1865, without fuss, without following, almost without being noticed. And the brief memorandum of his thoughts at the time, jotted down in shorthand for no eye but his own, has for me the heroic quality we associate with the records of Antarctic exploration. It concludes with these words: "I now believe in nothing, to put it shortly; but I do not the less believe in morality, etc., etc. I mean to live and die like a gentleman if possible."[1]

Then there is Stephen the nature-lover. He knew the Alps as well as any other man of his time; and no one who has read *The Playground of Europe*, which contains "The Alps in Winter" and "Sunset on Mont Blanc", two of the most satisfying descriptions of mountain

[1] *Life*, p. 144.

scenery in the language, can have failed to observe the affinity with Wordsworth. Not that Stephen is in the least derivative; at times he seems even to resent the thought of Wordsworth at his elbow, and turns, as it were, to exorcise his spirit. He has scaled the heights by his own efforts and skill, and worships the divinity in his own right and with his own eyes. Yet the divinity is the same, and the posture of the two men strikingly similar. Wordsworth speaks of

> a sense sublime
> Of something far more deeply interfused,
> Whose dwelling is the light of setting suns,
> And the round ocean and the living air,
> And the blue sky and in the mind of man.

And Stephen asks:

Where does Mont Blanc end, and where do I begin? That is the question which no metaphysician has hitherto succeeded in answering. But at least the connection is close and intimate. He is a part of the great machinery in which my physical frame is inextricably involved, and not the less interesting because a part which I am unable to subdue to my purposes. The whole universe, from the stars and the planets to the mountains and the insects which creep about their roots, is but a network of forces eternally acting and reacting upon each other. The mind of man is a musical instrument upon which all external objects are beating out infinitely complex harmonies and discords.[1]

Or take this picture of the Jungfrau in moonlight:

It was not a single mass—a flat continuous surface, as it often appears in the more emphatic lights and shades of daytime—but a whole wilderness of peak, cliff, and glacier, rising in terrace above terrace, and pyramid above pyramid, divided by mysterious valleys and shadowy recesses, the forms growing more delicate as they rose, till they culminated in the grand contrast of the balanced cone of the Silberhorn and the flowing sweep of the loftiest crest. A chaos of grand forms, it yet suggests some pervading design, too subtle to be understood by mortal vision, and scorning

[1] *The Playground of Europe*, pp. 260–1.

all comparison with earthly architecture. And the whole was formed, not of vulgar ice and earth, but of incarnate light. The darkest shadow was bright against the faint cliffs of the shadowy gorge, and the highest light faint enough to be woven out of reflected moonshine. So exquisitely modulated, and at once so audacious and so delicate in its sumptuous splendours of design, it belonged to the dream region, in which we appear to be inspired with supernatural influences.[1]

Cast this into blank verse, raise its temperature a few degrees, and you would have something very like one of the inspired passages of *The Excursion*.

Without question there was a close spiritual kinship between the gaunt athlete "like Wagner's *Flying Dutchman*" who made glad the hearts of men as tutor of this college from 1854 to 1864, and that other untidy, "gaunt and Don Quixote-like" figure, also "one of the best walkers and mountain climbers of his

[1] *The Playground of Europe*, pp. 301–2.

day", who after spending three years of terms watching

>the light of evening fade
Upon the silent Cam,

returned to find among the hills and sounding cataracts of his native Cumberland material for the creation of the greatest of modern English poetry.

Wordsworth speaks slightingly in *The Prelude* of the Cambridge curriculum, and of his official teachers. But he found here teachers of another sort, and of them he writes:

Beside the pleasant Mills of Trumpington
I laugh'd with Chaucer; in the hawthorn shade
Heard him (while birds were warbling) tell his tales
Of amorous passion. And that gentle Bard,
Chosen by the Muses for their Page of State,
Sweet Spenser, moving through his clouded heaven
With the moon's beauty and the moon's soft pace,
I call'd him Brother, Englishman, and Friend.
Yea, our blind Poet, who, in his later day,
Stood almost single, uttering odious truth,
Darkness before, and danger's voice behind;

Soul awful! if the earth has ever lodg'd
An awful Soul, I seem'd to see him here
Familiarly, and in his Scholar's dress
Bounding before me, yet a stripling Youth,
A Boy, no better, with his rosy cheeks
Angelical, keen eye, courageous look,
And conscious step of purity and pride.[1]

With the air full of such voices, is it surprising
that his destiny first dawned upon Wordsworth during his Cambridge years, though
the actual hour of dedication occurred in time
of vacation? We may claim him ours by
right. Cambridge too first recognised his
genius, and it is my thesis this afternoon that
Cambridge critics have been juster to him
than those of another place—a dangerous topic
for a Cambridge man to handle before a Cambridge audience, I admit; though the Vice-
Chancellor will perhaps remember Oxford
well enough to see fair play! But let us first
hear Leslie Stephen himself on the difference
between the two universities, a difference,

[1] *The Prelude* (1805 text), III, 276–93.

which, I fancy, has not yet disappeared. In a review of a *Life of Jowett*, published in 1897, he observes:

An interesting essay might, I fancy, be written upon the nature and origin of the difference between the Oxford and Cambridge spirit. Whatever the cause, one distinction is marked. Oxford has long been fertile in prophets; in men who cast a spell over a certain number of disciples, and not only pro-pagate ideas, but exercise a personal sway. At Cambridge no such leader, so far as I can remember, presented himself in my time; and, moreover, Cambridge men were generally inclined to regard their apparent barrenness with a certain complacency. Spiritual guides are troublesome personages. A prophet, per-haps, we thought, is apt to be a bit of a humbug, and at any rate a cause of humbug in others.... The opposite view is indicated by a remark of Jowett's upon Dr Arnold. Arnold had his weak points intellectually, says Jowett, "but in that one respect of inspiring others with ideals, there has been no one like him in modern times".

And having thus passed from Oxford to Rugby, Stephen enjoys himself in a brief but pleasant digression upon the Arnold tradition, which is as excellent as anything that Strachey has written upon it. Listen to this for example:

A conscience is, no doubt, a very useful possession in early years. But when a man has kept one till middle life, he ought to have established a certain *modus vivendi* with it; it should be absorbed and become part of himself—not a separate faculty delivering oracular utterances.[1]

What is Strachey's *Eminent Victorians* but a series of variations upon that theme? Indeed, the more we read of Stephen, the clearer grows our appreciation of Strachey's debt to him. The limpid style, the irony, the appetent smile with which Strachey exhibits to the reader the more delightful absurdities of a moral tumour before he lances it, all are to be

[1] *Studies of a Biographer*, II, pp. 125–8. Mr Mac-Carthy, I observe, quotes from another part of the same paragraph.

found in essay after essay of Leslie Stephen's volumes; and if there be any younger member of this audience gravelled for matter in literary research I commend to his attention the obligations of the debunking school of modern biography to the first editor of *The Dictionary of National Biography*, whose motto was "No flowers, by request". Strachey himself would, I believe, have acknowledged the debt with pride.

But to return to my theme, which is—to come at it more nearly—a discussion of the different views of Wordsworth's poetry held by Stephen and that finest flower of Rugby-cum-Oxford "moral consciousness", Matthew Arnold, son and heir of the great Doctor himself. The vicissitudes in opinion about Wordsworth, man and poet, since the publication of the *Lyrical Ballads* a hundred and forty years ago, form one of the curiosities of literary history, and the final chapter has yet to be written. In the main a confused spectacle of currents and cross-currents, it presents two conspicuous turning-points. One is the publication in 1897 of M. Legouis' *La Jeunesse de Wordsworth*, the effect of which has only been strengthened and completed by Professor Harper's revelation of the love-affair in France, first given us in 1916, and by Professor de Selincourt's discovery and publication ten years later of the 1805 text of *The Prelude*. All this did much to challenge the conception of "Daddy Wordsworth" entertained but not invented by Tennyson and Fitzgerald, who coined the phrase, a conception which passed current for fifty years after Wordsworth's death in 1850. Suddenly at the beginning of this century the world came to realise that the Wordsworth they read, the author of the only poems of his they bothered about, had been a young man, of strong passions and advanced opinions, which a few years before the composition of the poems in question led to an entanglement with a French girl and to political affinities with the Girondins which narrowly missed bringing him to the guillotine.

Some have attempted to reconcile the new with the old Wordsworth after the fashion of Mr Bertrand Russell, who writes in an essay entitled "The Harm that Good Men can do":

In his youth he sympathized with the French Revolution, went to France, wrote good poetry, and had a natural daughter. At this period he was a "bad" man. Then he became "good", abandoned his daughter, adopted correct principles, and wrote bad poetry.

Miss Edith Batho, from whose helpful, if at times exasperating, book I cull this gem, has little difficulty in showing it to be of paste, compounded of ignorance and prejudice; the truth being, as I do not need to remind you, that Wordsworth never "abandoned" his daughter, did not begin to write "good" poetry until he had ceased to "sympathize with the French Revolution", and continued till the end of his days both to write some "good" poetry and to entertain some radical principles. He was, in fact, as we are coming more and more to see, not only a great poet, but also a man of profound and independent mind; one of those central minds which belong to no party and no creed, but to which people of all creeds and parties turn for wisdom and strength. Burke was such a mind; Shakespeare, could we pronounce more definitely upon him, would seem to have been another.

I find it strange, then, that Matthew Arnold, to whom this type of mind was particularly attractive, should so utterly have missed detecting it in Wordsworth. Is it possible that the Rugby boy and the young Oxford man—for Wordsworth died while Arnold was still at his most dandified period—found the recluse at Rydal Mount too provincial, too uncultured for his tastes? It is at any rate recorded that once, over dinner at the Athenaeum, Arnold assured John Morley that Wordsworth was "too much of the peasant", or, even more bluntly, a "boor".[1] He would, no doubt, be annoyed

[1] These two expressions, both reported by Morley, evidently belong to different versions of the same

could he know that the casual word had escaped into history. Yet from a cosy corner of the Athenaeum, with brilliant talk passing to and fro across good wine and choice food, remembrance of "the rough grey face" of the Cumberland poet, "full of rifts and clefts and fissures, on which . . you might expect lichens to grow",[1] and of the Northern burr of his speech might seem to justify such an epithet. But there was more behind the expression than memories of the external man. It is evident that Arnold, son of the headmaster who had revolutionised English upper class education, and himself working day in and day out to extend the benefits of that revolution to the benighted middle classes, regarded the "Venerable Poet" at Rydal as the relic of a past age, of the rude uncivilised period

story, the more polite one being for Gladstone's ears. Miss Batho (p. 9) makes two stories out of them, and wrongly attributes one to C. H. Herford, who however clearly associates his version with Morley (*v.* his *Wordsworth*, p. 219).

[1] Herford, *op. cit.* p. 219.

before "Papa" went to Rugby to undertake the taming of the Barbarians. In other words, he thought of Wordsworth much as Dryden thought of Shakespeare; he looked upon him as a primitive, a great but untutored genius, to be admired but not imitated. Already in the first of his *Essays in Criticism* he was writing:

The English poetry of the first quarter of this century, with plenty of energy, plenty of creative force, did not know enough. This makes Byron so empty of matter, Shelley so incoherent, Wordsworth even, profound as he is, yet so wanting in completeness and variety. Wordsworth cared little for books, and disparaged Goethe. I admire Wordsworth, as he is, so much that I cannot wish him different....But surely the one thing wanting to make Wordsworth an even greater poet than he is—his thought richer, and his influence of wider application—was that he should have read more books, among them, no doubt, those of that Goethe whom he disparaged without reading him.[1]

[1] *Essays in Criticism*, I, p. 7.

He "disparaged Goethe"! Nothing more needed to be said. For Arnold, like Dryden, looked to the continent for his masters and his models, and to Arnold the greatest of these was Goethe. Had not Goethe, indeed, himself declared "Lord Byron is only great as a poet—directly he reflects he is a child"? Arnold's verdict upon Wordsworth was of the same pattern: he was, when inspired, a poet, "one of the very chief glories of English Poetry"; but he "did not know enough"—directly he tried to think he became a peasant.

Such was the mood in which the famous Preface on Wordsworth was written fifteen years later, a mood which had strengthened rather than weakened in the interim. The Preface forms an introduction to *Poems of Wordsworth, chosen and edited by Matthew Arnold*, published in the Golden Treasury series in 1879; and the appearance of the volume marks the other great turning-point in tide of Wordsworth's reputation of which I have spoken. As critic and editor Arnold set himself to a threefold task, which yet seemed to him one: he desired, in the first place, to disengage the best of Wordsworth's poems "from the quantity of inferior work which now obscures them"; in the second, to rescue the poet from the hands of a coterie of Wordsworthians, who were absurdly exalting him to the throne of poet-philosopher, side by side with the all-highest Goethe himself; and in the third, to demonstrate that his true greatness lay in his nature lyrics, and in his "style of perfect plainness" wherein, as Arnold puts it, echoing Dryden's words on the style of Shakespeare,[1] "Nature herself seems to take the pen out of his hand, and to write for him with her own bare, sheer, penetrating power". Finally, in casting about for the secret of Wordsworth's

[1] W. P. Ker, *Essays of John Dryden*, I, pp. 79–80: "All the images of Nature were still present to him, and he drew them, not laboriously, but luckily; when he describes anything, you more than see it, you feel it too.... He was naturally learned; he needed not the spectacles of books to read Nature; he looked inwards and found her there."

superiority over most other modern poets, English and continental, he arrived at the following conclusion:

Wordsworth's poetry is great because of the extraordinary power with which Wordsworth feels the joy offered to us in nature, the joy offered to us in the simple primary affections and duties; and because of the extraordinary power with which, in case after case, he shows us this joy, and renders it so as to make us share it.

The source of joy from which he thus draws is the truest and most unfailing source of joy accessible to man. It is also accessible universally. Wordsworth brings us word, therefore, according to his own strong and characteristic line, he brings us word

Of joy in widest commonalty spread.

Here is an immense advantage for a poet. Wordsworth tells us of what all seek, and tells us of it at its truest and best source, and yet a source where all may go and draw for it.[1]

It was a great moment in the history of our understanding of Wordsworth when Arnold

[1] *Preface*, p. xxi.

penned this passage. True, it merely expressed notions he had himself long entertained and to which he gave utterance in the elegiac verses commemorating Goethe, Byron and Wordsworth, when Wordsworth died in April 1850. The verses are as well known as the prose just quoted; yet I must quote them too if only to remind you of their loveliness:

> He too upon a wintry clime
> Had fallen—on this iron time
> Of doubts, disputes, distractions, fears.
> He found us when the age had bound
> Our soul in its benumbing round;
> He spoke, and loosed our heart in tears.
> He laid us as we lay at birth
> On the cool flowery lap of earth:
> Smiles broke from us and we had ease;
> The hills were round us, and the breeze
> Went o'er the sun-lit fields again;
> Our foreheads felt the wind and rain.
> Our youth returned; for there was shed
> On spirits that had long been dead,
> Spirits dried up and closely furled,
> The freshness of the early world.

No one before had seen Wordsworth quite in this light. As a poet Arnold might appear to be indulging in poetic fancy; but when the critic made the same point in prose, what he said was found so true, so simple and so obvious, that it seemed to leave nothing else to say. The criticism, indeed, has held English criticism spell-bound for sixty years, almost that is up to our own day. John Morley, for example, in his Introduction to the popular Macmillan edition of Wordsworth published in 1888, does little more than repeat and embroider Arnold's conclusions. As far as I know the only important book on Wordsworth, appearing before the Great War, which takes a different line, is that of Walter Raleigh, a Cambridge critic writing before he accepts an Oxford chair! who significantly enough does not mention Arnold's edition at all. Arnold's conclusion explains for all time one of the principal secrets of Wordsworth's attraction; but it is not a complete statement of the causes of his greatness, or even of his hold over our imagination. It is concerned solely with Wordsworth's feeling, with a single feeling, that of joy. It says nothing at all of other feelings, or of his ideas.

Until Arnold wrote, Wordsworth's ideas had, on the whole, been taken seriously by the world, especially, Arnold is careful to note, in this university.[1] But Arnold, as we have seen, possessed an ill-concealed contempt for Wordsworth's ideas; when he calls him "profound" he is thinking of the depth of his feeling. And since one of the principal objects of his edition was to rescue Wordsworth from the Cambridge Wordsworthians, the Professor of Poetry at Oxford spends the first three-quarters of his *Preface* in getting the ideas out of the way. In this undertaking he had two obstacles to surmount, both formidable to a critic less able and less confident than Arnold. The first was that Wordsworth himself happened to be the earliest Wordsworthian, inasmuch as he claimed to be primarily a

[1] *V.* the opening paragraph of the *Preface*.

philosophical poet, and even arranged his poems in a manner which would illustrate his ideas. Arnold never really troubles to examine either the claim or the arrangement. Of the latter he remarks: "His categories are ingenious but far-fetched, and the result of his employment of them unsatisfactory. Poems are separated one from another which possess a kinship of subject or of treatment far more vital and deep than the supposed unity of mental origin which was Wordsworth's reason for joining them with others."[1] To which I need only reply that Arnold's own arrangement is open to still graver criticism, and is to me at least entirely unhelpful. As for the claim, he calmly dismisses it as an illusion. Never has a great poet's self-estimate been more lightly disposed of by a serious critic.

The other obstacle in Arnold's path was not so easily circumvented, since it lay in the central doctrine of his own critical theory, viz. that literature is great in proportion as it

[1] *Preface*, pp. xii–xiii.

succeeds in combining style with a profound "criticism of life". One would naturally suppose that no poet answered better to this prescription than Wordsworth, and it is clever of Arnold, at the outset of his *Preface*, to let us imagine that he intends leading us in that direction, since it makes the conclusion, when it comes, all the more effective by its very surprise.

A great poet (he begins by saying) receives his distinctive character of superiority from his application, under the conditions immutably fixed by the laws of poetic beauty and poetic truth, from his application, I say, to his subject, whatever it may be, of the ideas

On man, on nature, and on human life,

which he has acquired for himself. The line quoted is Wordsworth's own; and his superiority arises from his powerful use, in his best pieces, his powerful application to his subject, of ideas "on man, on nature, and on human life".[1]

[1] *Preface*, p. xiv.

Yet five pages further on he is writing:

We must be on our guard against the Wordsworthians, if we want to secure for Wordsworth his due rank as a poet. The Wordsworthians are apt to praise him for the wrong things, and to lay far too much stress upon what they call his philosophy. His poetry is the reality, his philosophy—so far, at least, as it may put on the form and habit of "a scientific system of thought", and the more that it puts them on—is the illusion. Perhaps we shall one day learn to make this proposition general, and to say: Poetry is the reality, philosophy the illusion. But in Wordsworth's case, at any rate, we cannot do him justice until we dismiss his formal philosophy.[1]

How does Arnold reconcile these two positions? He does not attempt to. On the contrary, after laughing at the Wordsworthians for seeking in Wordsworth for "a scientific system of thought", he suddenly rounds upon them with his passage about joy, concludes with a discussion of the poet's style and says

[1] *Ibid.* pp. xviii–xix.

nothing more about ideas or "the criticism of life" whatever. It is perhaps the most audacious *non sequitur* in the annals of English criticism.

Now the only Wordsworthian Arnold mentions by name is Leslie Stephen. Arnold is one of those writers who can seldom get moving across country without first putting up an opponent; and the exhilaration of the chase—nothing more vicious than that—sometimes leads him to play tricks with his quarry. He had made up his mind to rescue Wordsworth from the Wordsworthians, and an essay by Leslie Stephen, entitled *Wordsworth's Ethics*, which had appeared a few months before in *Hours in a Library* (series III), provided Arnold with exactly the text he was on the look-out for, though there is no evidence that he had read anything more of it than the following paragraph:

Other poetry becomes trifling when we are making our inevitable passages through the Valley of the Shadow of Death. Wordsworth's alone retains its power. We love him the more as we grow older and become more deeply impressed with the sadness and seriousness of life; we are apt to grow weary of his rivals when we have finally quitted the regions of youthful enchantment. And I take the explanation to be that he is not merely a melodious writer, or a powerful utterer of deep emotion, but a true philosopher. His poetry wears well, because it has solid substance. He is a prophet and a moralist, as well as a mere singer. His ethical system, in particular, is as distinctive and capable of systematic exposition as that of Butler. By endeavouring to state it in plain prose, we shall see how the poetical power implies a sensitiveness to ideas which, when extracted from the symbolical embodiment, fall spontaneously into a scientific system.[1]

"He is a prophet and a moralist, as well as a *mere* singer" is not a very happy way of putting things, while the notion of "extracting" a poet's "ideas from the symbolical embodiment" hardly falls in with modern critical

[1] *Hours in a Library,* 1879, III, pp. 187-8.

notions. Neither, however, caught the attention of Arnold. What he fastened upon was the thesis that Wordsworth's ideas

On man, on nature, and on human life,

were capable of "systematic exposition"; it was so exactly what a Cambridge man *would* say! And, then, after quoting one of the less inspired passages from *The Excursion* by way of exhibiting the peasant "philosopher" in action, he continues:

Wordsworth calls Voltaire dull, and surely the production of these un-Voltairian lines must have been imposed on him as a judgment! One can hear them being quoted at a Social Science Congress; one can call up the whole scene. A great room in one of our dismal provincial towns; dusty air and jaded afternoon daylight; benches full of men with bald heads and women in spectacles; an orator lifting up his face from a manuscript written within and without to declaim these lines of Wordsworth; and in the soul of any poor child of nature who may have wandered in thither, an unutterable sense of lamentation, and mourning, and woe! "But turn we", as Wordsworth says, "from these bold, bad men", the haunters of Social Science Congresses. And let us be on our guard, too, against the exhibitors and extollers of a "scientific system of thought" in Wordsworth's poetry.[1]

It is sallies like this which specially delighted readers of Arnold's own generation, and embalm more mortal parts of his prose writings for the delectation of ours. How it recreates for us the atmosphere of progressive Victorian England, the very smell of it! It is also an impish attack upon Leslie Stephen. For the suggestion clearly is that Stephen and Social Science Congresses[2] belong together, that Stephen is the orator with the uplifted face intoning the duller passages from Wordsworth, while the child of nature with soul full of lamentation and woe presumably stands for Arnold himself. In fact, it illustrates, as

[1] *Preface*, p. xxi.
[2] Stephen's real attitude towards such assemblies may be seen in *Sketches from Cambridge*, p. 41 (ed. 1932).

Stephen says of another of Arnold's articles, "Mat in excelsis". For what could be more deliciously impertinent than for this diner-out, this lion of society, this "elaborate Jeremiah", this denouncer of Wordsworth's boorishness in the fastnesses of the Athenaeum, to pose as "a child of nature", unless it be that such a child should pretend to have been outraged by the conqueror of the Schreckhorn, the leader of the Sunday Tramps, the model of Vernon Whitford in *The Egoist*? Yet Stephen, no doubt, smiled at "Mat's cheekiness", as he read it, and forgave him, if it ever occurred to him that forgiveness was needed.[1] For he admired the great Matthew, this side idolatry, as much as any; and he was incapable of bearing malice.

"But turn we from this bold, bad Arnold" to consider Stephen's essay and the claims it

---

[1] For Stephen's views upon Arnold, the reader should turn to his essay on him, the most delightful of the *Studies of a Biographer* (II, pp. 76 ff.). If only we had one by Arnold upon Stephen to set beside it!

makes more closely. "What Mr Wordsworth *will* produce, it is not for me to prophesy", Coleridge had declared in the *Biographia Literaria*; "but I could pronounce with the liveliest conviction what he is capable of producing. It is the FIRST GENUINE PHILOSOPHICAL POEM."[1] Such was the opinion, emphasised by capital letters, of the contemporary who knew Wordsworth's mind best, and himself possessed a profoundly philosophical mind. There was nothing, then, either new or frivolous in Stephen's claim; rather it was Arnold's attempt to rid Wordsworth of his philosophical baggage which was the innovation. Coleridge was writing in 1817, three years after *The Excursion* appeared, and his confident prophecy was based upon his knowledge of that poem and of *The Prelude*. That Wordsworth never, largely (as Miss Batho has shown) because of his defective eyesight, fulfilled the prophecy, is nothing to the matter. What he called, in his Preface to *The Excursion*,

[1] Ed. Shawcross, II, p. 129.

"the body of" his "Gothic church" may be lacking, but we have "the ante-chapel", together with the shorter poems which "when they shall be properly arranged, will be found by the attentive reader to have such connection with the main work as may give them claim to be likened to the little cells, oratories, and sepulchral recesses, ordinarily included in those edifices". Arnold despised and destroyed this architectural plan, now happily restored in the Oxford text. Yet even his fragmentary and disarranged edition contains many poems which cannot be explained on his own "simple" theory. A consistent body of ideas is certainly discoverable "by the attentive reader" in Wordsworth's poetry; and Stephen's pioneer attempt to set it forth in 1879 has been followed up in 1922 by Professor Beatty, whose *William Wordsworth: his doctrine and art in their historical relations*[1] proves without

[1] That this able book is unappetising in appearance and laboured in execution has hindered its due recognition. It needs digesting and completing by a first-rate critic.

possibility of contradiction that the poet worked upon a clearly conceived and articulated psychology of the developing human being in his relation to the external world of nature.

> The child is father to the man,
> And I could wish my days to be
> Bound each to each by natural piety,

is the motto Wordsworth chose to set at the head of his poetical works, and everything he writes is an illustration of it. "Wordsworth's philosophical theory, in short", said Stephen, "depends upon the asserted identity between our childish instincts and our enlightened reason." It depends upon the recognition of what may be called a hierarchy in human experience, and if we are to be "an attentive reader", that is, to understand what Wordsworth desires to tell us, it is of first importance that we should know of what particular stage, or stages, of growth he is speaking at any given moment. How else can we follow even the main drift of poems like *Lines above Tintern Abbey* or the *Ode on Intimations of Immortality*, in which the poet, standing as it were on the eminence of an intensely felt experience, looks before and after; contemplating the dissolving views of past experiences, and comparing them with the feelings of the present and hopes of the future?

Yet it is not too much to say that "attentive" reading of this kind is hardly ever accorded to Wordsworth. The common notion, for example, that he is a second Vaughan, constantly sounding his "Retreat", perpetually moaning over something lost in the past, is only one of the grosser forms of error into which people fall who, following Arnold's advice, read him as a lyric poet, and neglect his psychology. G. K. Chesterton speaks in one of his books, though where I have forgotten, of "the blasphemy" of those lines in the *Ode* on "the vision splendid" which conclude

At length the Man perceives it die away,
And fade into the light of common day.

As if Wordsworth did not spend a whole lifetime in hymning just that "light of common day" which Chesterton, taking the passage out of its context and ignoring even the conclusion of the *Ode* itself, vainly imagines that he despises! This and not

The light that never was, on sea or land,
The consecration, and the Poet's dream,

was what Wordsworth lived by and for. Yet these lines again, lines which occur in the *Elegiac Stanzas*, written after the death of John Wordsworth at sea, are almost invariably misapprehended. It is astonishing how few readers seem to notice that the poet immediately afterwards calls "the light that never was" a "fond illusion", and concludes the poem as follows:

Farewell, farewell the heart that lives alone,
Housed, in a dream, at distance from the Kind!
Such happiness, wherever it be known,
Is to be pitied; for 'tis surely blind.

But welcome fortitude, and patient cheer,
And frequent sights of what is to be borne!

Such sights, or worse, as are before me here.—
Not without hope we suffer and we mourn.

Even Coleridge himself was inattentive enough
to identify Wordsworth's imagination with
this "fond illusion". Little wonder that in
despair Wordsworth revised the lines, and
utterly spoilt them in the process! And where
Coleridge nods, we ought not to be surprised,
I suppose, to find, a modern disciple of his,
a philosophical critic like Dr Richards, occa-
sionally tripping. But it was, I must confess,
a little startling to note that the long and
helpful disquisition on the relation between
Nature and Mind in Wordsworth's poems,
which he gives us in his book on Coleridge,
contains no reference whatever to the well-
known lines:

Therefore am I still
A lover of the meadows and the woods,
And mountains; and of all that we behold
From this green earth; of all the mighty world
Of eye and ear, *both what they half create,*
And what perceive

—lines which surely decide for us the question whether Wordsworth took the "realist" or the "projective" view of the universe, by showing that he entertained both at the same time. Such oversights could not occur had criticism ever faced the easy and elementary task which Stephen suggested in 1879 might be undertaken, viz. the "systematic exposition" of Wordsworth's leading ideas. Is it not time that we should close our Matthew Arnolds and perform this simple service for our Cambridge poet?

But what, it may be asked, would be the value of Wordsworth's philosophy if we recovered it? Is it not pre-Darwinian, and therefore hopelessly out of date? "His conception of nature as a living and sentient and benignant being", declared the Leslie Stephen lecturer of 1933, is "a conception as purely mythological as the Dryads and the Naiads".[1] Or listen to the voice of a grandson of that

[1] A. E. Housman, *The Name and Nature of Poetry*, p. 35.

Thomas Huxley, who found himself compelled to put asunder the ethical process and the cosmic process which Wordsworth had joined together:

In the neighbourhood of latitude fifty north, and for the last hundred years or thereabouts, it has been an axiom that Nature is divine and morally uplifting.... The Wordsworthian who exports this pantheistic worship of Nature to the tropics is liable to have his religious convictions somewhat rudely disturbed. Nature, under a vertical sun, and nourished by the equatorial rains, is not at all like that chaste, mild deity who presides over the Gemüthlichkeit, the prettiness, the cosy sublimities of the Lake District.[1]

This type of objection, though plausible at first blush, has always seemed to me a superficial one. Mr Aldous Huxley's cosy Cumberland is the Lakeland of motors and metalled roads, seen through modern eyes, in summer time. The "sublimities" may still be grim

[1] Aldous Huxley, "Wordsworth in the Tropics" (*What you will*, p. 113).

enough in wild weather, while one has only to read the opening chapter of Stephen's *Playground of Europe* to realise that most people a hundred and fifty years ago felt about European mountains very much what Mr Huxley now feels about the tropics. So quickly indeed does human sentiment concerning natural scenery change that long before another hundred and fifty years are passed, when the tropics will have become habitable, we may very well see a black Wordsworth chanting the glories of the West African swamps. As to "nature red in tooth and claw", Stephen was already facing that in 1879, and remarks: "To say that Wordsworth has not given a complete answer to such difficulties, is to say that he has not explained the origin of evil."[1] Had Wordsworth been able to read Darwin, he might perhaps have used a rather different language. But that the theory of natural selection would have caused him to shift a hair's breadth from his main position I do not

[1] *Hours in a Library*, III, pp. 199–201.

for a moment believe. On the contrary, it must have deepened his sense of the oneness of man with nature, and of the "whole creation groaning and travailing in pain together".

But what Stephen does not say, because at that date he could not realise, and what these modern objectors overlook without his excuse, is that there was very little that was "cosy" in the spectacle of man and nature which confronted Wordsworth when he began writing. Newton had demonstrated that the universe was a piece of dead mechanism; Locke had done much the like with human nature;[1] while as for man's ideals and hopes, they had after the brief exhilaration of the revolutionary dawn been tumbled in the blood and sawdust of the Reign of Terror and trampled underfoot by the Napoleonic wars. Unless we grasp that background, we are liable to misjudge Wordsworth altogether. He wrote just because to

[1] Cf. B. Willey, *The Seventeenth-Century Background*, ch. xii.

his generation the problem of evil seemed so formidable; he wrote to save the world from despair; he wrote because he had himself found, as he believed, the secret of happiness after years of bitterness and agony of spirit. And how like the background is to ours! How well did this English Girondin know the heart-sickness and crucifixion of mind which afflict us to-day! After the Terror, he tells us,

Through months, through years,
I scarcely had one night of quiet sleep,
Such ghastly visions had I of despair
And tyranny, and implements of death,
And long orations which in dreams I pleaded
Before unjust Tribunals, with a voice
Labouring, a brain confounded, and a sense
Of treachery and desertion in the place
The holiest that I knew of, my own soul.

How many of us in this room have endured, still endure, that "sense of treachery and desertion in the place" of the soul, as we contemplate the brutalities of human nature in our

(51)

own world? Has not Wordsworth something then for us too?

Arnold did well to emphasise Wordsworth's joy. It is a point, as I have said, of first importance. One has only, for instance, to read the *Autobiography* of J. S. Mill to see how the sense of it could shed

> On spirits that had long been dead,
> Spirits dried up and closely furled,
> The freshness of the early world.

But joy is not the only thing in Wordsworth, and they who limit him to that do him great wrong. Here again Stephen's essay on *Wordsworth's Ethics* is of real help. Of joy it makes no mention: on the contrary the emphasis is all upon what Wordsworth says about pain and affliction, and of how they may be transmuted into moral strength. "All moral teaching", Stephen writes, "I have sometimes fancied, might be summed up in the one formula, 'Waste not'.... The waste of sorrow is one of the most lamentable forms of waste."[1]

[1] *Hours in a Library*, III, pp. 220–1.

And again: "Other poets mock us by an impossible optimism, or merely reflect the feelings which, however we may play with them in times of cheerfulness, have now become an intolerable burden. Wordsworth suggests the single topic which, as far at least as this world goes, can really be called consolatory."[1] And yet again: "Wordsworth has the merit of feeling the truth in all its force, and expressing it by the most forcible images."[2] Is not this as searching and as revealing as anything Arnold says on the subject

Of joy in widest commonalty spread?

And are not the two criticisms complementary? John Morley, who wears Arnold's blinkers, actually declares that "Wordsworth had not rooted in him the sense of Fate".[3] Can Morley, one asks, have read *The White Doe of Rylstone*, or *Michael*, or *The Ruined Cottage*, or *The Character of the Happy Warrior*,

[1] *Ibid.* p. 219.   [2] *Ibid.*
[3] Introduction to Macmillan's Wordsworth, p. lxvi.

or *The Prelude* itself? Wordsworth was not a dramatist; he gave us nothing to set beside *King Lear*. But he did not shirk the issues that *King Lear* raises. He did not, as Arnold asserts he did, "put by"

> The cloud of mortal destiny;

he fronted it as fearlessly as Shakespeare. Is there any other poem in the language which gives utterance, at once so ruthlessly and so bracingly, to the desolation of human grief, as

> A slumber did my spirit seal,
>   I had no human fears:
> She seemed a thing that could not feel
>   The touch of earthly years.
>
> No motion has she now, no force;
>   She neither hears nor sees,
> Rolled round in earth's diurnal course,
>   With rocks, and stones, and trees.

And what of those public griefs already touched upon? A poet whose best work was written between the dates 1798 and 1815 has much to say to a generation which finds itself once again entrusted with the task of thwarting

Napoleonic ambitions. One of the strangest
omissions in Arnold's Preface is that he makes
no mention of Wordsworth's "Poems dedi-
cated to National Independence and Liberty".
Rather than these, however, in the brief time
still left to me, I would call to mind the poem
which, perhaps above all others, exemplifies
the truth of Stephen's criticism; I mean that
on the *Happy Warrior*,

Who, doomed to go in company with Pain,
And Fear, and Bloodshed, miserable train!
Turns his necessity to glorious gain;
In face of these doth exercise a power
Which is our human nature's highest dower;
Controls them and subdues, transmutes, be-
    reaves
Of their bad influence, and their good receives:
By objects, which might force the soul to abate
Her feeling, rendered more compassionate.

And have not these lines also a special meaning
for our age?

But who, if he be called upon to face
Some awful moment to which Heaven has
    joined

Great issues, good or bad for human kind,
Is happy as a lover; and attired
With sudden brightness, like a man inspired;
And through the heat of conflict, keeps the law
In calmness made, and sees what he foresaw.

But I am afraid that all this talk about
Wordsworth's moral ideas will sound very
old-fashioned in the ears of some present.
"Poetry", one of our modern masters has
declared, "is not the thing said, but a way of
saying it".[1] And another, of quite a different
school, assures us that the truth or falsity of
a poet's statements or beliefs ought to be a
matter of complete indifference to the reader.[2]
Yet the poets themselves remain incorrigible.
I have not observed that our younger singers,
discharging their ideological verses at each
other's heads from opposite sides of the
Spanish trenches, regard their own beliefs
with indifference; while having once spent a

[1] A. E. Housman, *op. cit.* p. 37.
[2] I. A. Richards, *Principles of Literary Criticism*, ch. xxxv.

memorable hour listening to Mr T. S. Eliot reciting his poetry, I was left with the abiding impression that his object, not less than Wordsworth's, was "truth carried alive into the heart by passion". And readers I fear, in this country at any rate, are likely to remain as incorrigible as poets. No doubt a great poet like Tennyson, who narrowed his poetic vision too often to the moral horizon of his own generation, will run the risk of being scorned by the inevitable rebels of the next. But with Wordsworth it is otherwise. A Cambridge critic, Mr Willey, has shown how entirely original he was,[1] and Professor A. N. Whitehead, another Cambridge man, whom some think the greatest of living philosophers, has ranked him among the major forces still at work in the formation of modern thought.[2] The ideas of Wordsworth, his statements and his beliefs, will see us out our time.

[1] B. Willey, *The Seventeenth-Century Background*, ch. XII.
[2] *Science and the Modern World*, ch. v.

But if, following in Leslie Stephen's steps, I have pleaded for the further study of them, let me conclude with a word of caution. Wordsworth is as free and, except for his lack of humour, as broad as the English spirit. He is not to be shut up into any of our conventicles, philosophical or ecclesiastic. And by "Wordsworth" I mean the poet of 1798–1815, the Wordsworth of the best period. I have shown how even Matthew Arnold went astray by attempting to limit him to one aspect of his appeal. A mission has recently been launched, strangely enough from the monument of Jeremy Bentham in Gower Street, London, for the reclamation of all poets with theologies not otherwise identifiable to the Anglo-Catholic fold. Professors Sisson and R. W. Chambers have done their best, or their worst, with Shakespeare; and now Miss Edith Batho, a member of their school, has tried her hand on Wordsworth. I have read her book with interest; often, as you will have observed, with enlightenment; never, I hope,

(58)

with prejudice, seeing that I am myself an unworthy member of the Church for which she proselytises. But I remain unconvinced, and I confess I am glad of it. For Wordsworth belongs to us all, to leaders of the Oxford Movement like John Keble, to unitarians like Stopford Brooke, to the "saints of rationalism" like John Stuart Mill and Leslie Stephen. At the height of his powers, he was, as I have said, one of those great central minds, which are the property of no party and of no creed, but to which people of all creeds and parties turn for beauty, for joy, for wisdom and for strength.